JAPANESE MYTHOLOGY

Kitsune

BY EMMA KAISER

CONTENT CONSULTANT
NAOMI FUKUMORI, PhD
ASSOCIATE PROFESSOR OF PREMODERN JAPANESE LITERATURE AND CULTURE
THE OHIO STATE UNIVERSITY

Kids Core
An Imprint of Abdo Publishing
abdobooks.com

abdobooks.com

Printed in the United States of America, North Mankato, Minnesota.
102024
012025

Cover Photo: Shutterstock Images
Interior Photos: Zoom Historical/Alamy, 4–5, 28 (bottom); Indianapolis Museum of Art at Newfields/Archive Photos/Getty Images, 7; Sepia Times/Universal Images Group/Getty Images, 8; Shutterstock Images, 10, 12–13, 15, 17 (top left), 17 (top middle), 17 (top right), 17 (middle left), 17 (middle), 17 (bottom left, bottom middle), 18, 28 (top); Hanna Udod/iStockphoto, 14; Maksim Ankuda/Shutterstock Images, 17 (middle right); Yana Lesnik/Shutterstock Images, 17 (bottom right); The Protected Art Archive/Alamy, 20–21, 29 (top); Planetpix/Alamy, 23; iStockphoto, 24, 29 (bottom); B. Tanaka/The Image Bank Unreleased/Getty Images, 26

Editor: Christa Kelly
Series Designer: Ryan Gale

Library of Congress Control Number: 2024938362

Publisher's Cataloging-in-Publication Data

Names: Kaiser, Emma, author.
Title: Kitsune / by Emma Kaiser
Description: Minneapolis, Minnesota: ABDO Publishing, 2025 | Series: Japanese mythology | Includes online resources and index.
Identifiers: ISBN 9781098295974 (lib. bdg.) | ISBN 9798384916970 (ebook)
Subjects: LCSH: Mythology, Japanese--Juvenile literature. | Deities--Juvenile literature. | Kitsune--Juvenile literature. | Foxes (in religion, folk-lore, etc.)--Juvenile literature. | Foxes--Folklore--Juvenile literature. | Tricksters--Juvenile literature. | Mythology, Asian--Juvenile literature.
Classification: DDC 398.21--dc23

CONTENTS

CHAPTER 1
The Legend of the White Fox 4

CHAPTER 2
The Power of the Kitsune 12

CHAPTER 3
Messengers of the Gods 20

Legendary Facts 28
Glossary 30
Online Resources 31
Learn More 31
Index 32
About the Author 32

The legend of the white fox is told in books, art, and plays.

CHAPTER 1

The Legend of the White Fox

There once was a man named Abe no Yasuna (pronounced ah-bay noh yahs-oo-nah). Yasuna was a **nobleman** in early Japan. One day, Yasuna was walking in the Shinoda Forest. A group of hunters ran by him. They were chasing a white fox.

Suddenly, the white fox dashed out from the trees. The fox looked at Yasuna, silently pleading with him for help. Yasuna hid the white fox in his robes. Once the hunters had passed, Yasuna let the fox go. The fox ran away into the forest.

Later, Yasuna met a beautiful young woman named Kuzunoha (kuz-oo-noh-ha). Yasuna and Kuzunoha fell in love and got married. They had a son. For years, the family was happy. But Kuzunoha had a secret. She was not really human. She was the white fox that Yasuna had saved.

Kuzunoha was not a normal fox. She was a magical creature called a *kitsune* (kit-soo-nay). Kitsune can **shape-shift**. Kuzunoha had disguised herself as a human. But one day, she

According to Japanese mythology, reflections and shadows show the true forms of monsters and spirits.

was careless with her disguise. Her young son caught a glimpse of her tail. Once her secret was discovered, she could not stay in her human form any longer.

Kuzunoha is often shown holding a brush in her mouth as she writes a note to her family.

Before she left, Kuzunoha visited her son one last time. She left a note on the door of her home. The note read, "If you think of me with love, come seek me in the forests." Then, she returned to the Shinoda Forest.

Her husband and son traveled to the forest to look for Kuzunoha. Finally, the white fox appeared to them one last time. Her family realized that Kuzunoha had been a kitsune all along.

Shinto

Japan is an island nation in East Asia. Many people in Japan practice a religion called Shinto. Shinto is the native religion of Japan.

The Shrine of Kuzunoha

There is a **shrine** in Osaka, Japan, dedicated to Kuzunoha. Osaka stands where the Shinoda Forest used to be. Because Kuzunoha was known as a loving mother, many parents come to the shrine to pray for their children.

Kitsune are important figures in Shinto mythology.

It centers around the worship of kami. The word *kami* means "spirits." Some kami are gods. Others are **mythical** creatures.

The Japanese word *kitsune* means "fox." Some of these foxes are normal animals.

Others are magical creatures. In English, the word *kitsune* usually refers to the magical foxes.

People in Japan have been telling stories about mythical creatures for more than 1,000 years. This mythology is an important part of Shinto. Many Japanese myths include kitsune. For hundreds of years, these creatures have fascinated the people of Japan.

Further Evidence

Look at the website below. Does it give any new evidence to support Chapter One?

Kuzunoha

abdocorelibrary.com/kitsune

Some kitsune are invisible, but people can see their reflections in water.

CHAPTER 2

The Power of the Kitsune

Though kitsune may look like foxes, they are powerful beings. Kitsune have many magical powers. They can shape-shift into other creatures. Kitsune are also very smart. They can live for hundreds of years.

Kitsune like to eat tofu and rice.

They become smarter and more powerful the longer they live.

As magical kitsune get older, they grow more tails. When a kitsune has lived 1,000 years, it grows its ninth tail. The kitsune then turns white or gold and flies up to the heavens.

There are two types of kitsune. Some are known as *zenko*. This means "good foxes."

According to Japanese folklore, any woman seen alone at night could be a kitsune.

These kitsune are messengers of the Shinto god Inari. They protect and help the god. These kitsune are sometimes worshipped as kami.

Other kitsune are known as *nogitsune*. This means "wild foxes." These kitsune are mischievous and known for playing tricks.

Shape-shifters

Kitsune can change how they look. By age 100, they are powerful enough to shape-shift into humans. To transform, they bow and place reeds or leaves over their heads. Usually, kitsune take the forms of women and girls. They use their disguises to trick men.

Spotting a Kitsune's Tail

One way to spot a kitsune in disguise is to look for its tails. Sometimes a kitsune is careless and reveals its tails while in human form.

The Powers of the Kitsune

Kitsune have many different magical abilities.

At night, kitsune make strange, ghostly lights called *kitsune-bi*.

Kitsune have other powers too. They can make fire and control lightning. They can fly and turn invisible. They also have power over humans. Sometimes kitsune enter people's dreams. Other times, they take over people's minds. They can also make people see things that aren't there. Some of the most powerful kitsune can even control time and space.

Primary Source

Guo Pu was a historian. He describes the powers of kitsune:

> When a fox is fifty years old, it can transform itself into a woman. When it is one hundred, it becomes . . . good at witchcraft, **beguiling** people and making them lose their senses. When they are a thousand years old, they . . . become heavenly foxes.

Source: Rania Huntington. *Alien Kind: Foxes and Late Imperial Chinese Narrative*. Harvard University Asia Center, 2003, p. 1.

What's the Big Idea?

Read the quote. What is its main idea? Explain how the main idea is supported by details.

In Chinese mythology, Tamamo no Mae, *top*, was an evil *huli jing* who made people sick.

CHAPTER 3

Messengers of the Gods

People in China have been telling stories about magical foxes for thousands of years. They called these creatures *huli jing.* The foxes had nine tails and could shape-shift. Some of the foxes were dangerous. Others were kind.

Stories about the *huli jing* eventually spread across Asia. The myths made their way into Japanese **culture**. As early as the 900s CE, Japanese stories were written about foxes having magical, godlike powers. The creatures became known as kitsune.

Kitsune and Inari

Kitsune are closely linked to the god Inari. Inari is the protector of rice. In Japanese folklore, kitsune deliver messages from Inari to humans. The foxes can be signs of good luck or of a good rice harvest.

There are many shrines built for Inari in Japan. These shrines often contain stone statues of foxes. The foxes represent kitsune.

The Toyokawa Inari shrine has 1,000 kitsune statues.

Kitsune statues often carry keys to Inari's rice storage.

Kitsune statues appear in more than 30,000 shrines throughout Japan. The foxes are usually seated, guarding the shrines. Each has a unique facial expression.

Sometimes kitsune statues wear red bibs. In Shinto, red is the color of the gods. The color scares off bad energy. Some of the fox statues also hold items in their mouths, such as keys, scrolls, or jewels.

The Inari Grand Shrine

The most important Inari shrine is located outside of Kyoto, Japan. It is called the Fushimi Inari Grand Shrine. The shrine is at the base of Mount Inari. People travel to the shrine to pray.

Kitsune appear in many theater performances. Actors and dancers portraying kitsune wear fox masks.

Kitsune in Art

Kitsune are popular characters in art. They are often shown as tricksters in Japanese theater. Kitsune also appear in many woodblock prints. Prints are made by carving an image into wood. The wood block is then dipped in ink. Paper is pressed onto the block to make a print.

Many woodblock prints show Kuzunoha being revealed as a kitsune.

Kitsune are also popular in modern pop culture. They appear in movies and television shows. Some video game characters are based on kitsune too. These include several characters from the *Pokémon* series. Long after their stories were first told, kitsune remain an important part of Japanese mythology.

Explore Online

Visit the website below. Does it give any new information about Inari and kitsune that wasn't in Chapter Three?

Kitsune and Tanuki

abdocorelibrary.com/kitsune

Legendary Facts

Magical kitsune look like foxes but have special powers.

Kitsune often transform into humans.

Some kitsune are helpers and signs of good luck. Others are tricksters.

Fox sculptures appear in more than 30,000 shrines around Japan.

Glossary

beguiling
tricking by being charming

culture
the beliefs and practices of a particular group of people

mythical
appearing in myths

nobleman
someone with an important title or rank

shape-shift
change from one shape to another, often transforming into different creatures

shrine
a place where gods and other religious figures are honored and worshipped

Online Resources

To learn more about kitsune and Japanese mythology, visit our free resource websites below.

Visit **abdocorelibrary.com** or scan this QR code for free Common Core resources for teachers and students, including vetted activities, multimedia, and booklinks, for deeper subject comprehension.

Visit **abdobooklinks.com** or scan this QR code for free additional online weblinks for further learning. These links are routinely monitored and updated to provide the most current information available.

Learn More

Fox, Jay. *My First Book of Japanese*. Bushel & Peck, 2022.

Lee, Jean Kuo. *Tengu*. Abdo, 2025.

Yasuda, Yuri. *Japanese Myths, Legends, and Folktales: Bilingual English and Japanese Edition*. Tuttle, 2019.

Index

China, 19, 21

Fushimi Inari Grand Shrine, 25

huli jing, 21–22

Inari, 15, 22, 25, 27

Kuzunoha, 5–9, 11, 27
Kyoto, 25

Mount Inari, 25

nogitsune, 16

Osaka, 9

powers, 6, 13–14, 16, 17, 18, 19, 22

Shinoda Forest, 5–6, 8, 9
Shinto, 9–11, 15, 22–25

Yasuna, Abe no, 5–6, 9

zenko, 14

About the Author

Emma Kaiser is a writer and educator based in western Minnesota. She has an MFA in creative writing from the University of Minnesota, and her writing has appeared in a number of magazines and publications. She is the author of a number of other nonfiction books for students.